HIS SECRET POWER

The International Dough Championship

ANNA NASSIF

His Secret Power
The International Dough Championship
by Anna Nassif

Published by Anna Nassif

ISBN: 978-0-6483142-0-2

Illustrations and cover page by Chloe Chin
www.facebook.com/bychloechin

Edit and layout by Kim Lambert Dreamstone Publishing
www.dreamstonepublishing.com

Phonetic transcription by Emilia Tarnowska

www.facebook.com/hissecretpower

Dla Eliasza, Antka i Zosi

- Mama

This is the day we have all been waiting for. A show like no other, the first international championship for dough.

The crowd is excited, everyone is keen,
Only five minutes to go, let's finally begin.

Backstage two Spanish dumplings are screaming at each other:

'Just look at your red face, no one will like you, so don't even bother!'

'They will all love me, but you, on the other hand,

should use better sunscreen, you are just too tanned!'

All of a sudden, rushing in with a bang
through the main theatre door,

is a crispy dumpling with a rolling pin -
who knows what he needs it for?

Tall and handsome, with a black moustache,
nobody saw him coming.

With his hat to one side and a cheeky grin,
could he take a lead in the running?

He looks around and, when he's done,
says with a loud voice, to everyone:

'Dzień dobry. Jestem Pieróg Włodek. Jak wam leci życie?
Witam wszystkich, widzę, że się tu bardzo dobrze bawicie.'

All the contestants froze in shock
to hear such funny talk.

But soon after,
pointing fingers at Włodek,
they all burst into laughter.

You'd think he'd have stopped his presentation.
But not Włodek, oh no!

All of a sudden,
Pieróg Włodek from Poland became a real sensation.

'Pochodzę z daleka' **the story goes on**
'z kraju, gdzie zima jest w grudniu,
a bzy kwitną w maju.
Gdzie gofry, pierniki i oscypki są dobrze znane
od Bałtyku przez Toruń aż po Zakopane.

Mój kraj rodzinny, Polskę, za dom uznają:
sarny, żubry, wilki i dziki, brunatne niedźwiedzie
oraz bociany, co czerwone dzioby mają...'

WAŁBRZYCH

WARSZAWA

Włodek was slowly drifting away
in the daydream he was having that day.
His thoughts of the country of his youth
made him so emotional
you could tell he was speaking the truth.

Suddenly his tale was cut short
when from the stage came a loud snort.

'The judges are here,' everyone started to whisper,
'I can see them already. Mr Pig, his wife and her sister.'

All the donuts, dumplings, and ravioli,

Noodles, wontons, croissants, cannelloni,

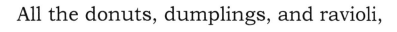

pancakes, brioche, even Russian blini,

bread, cookies and biscottini,

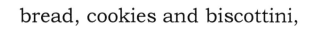

each of them in their glory

wants to win in their category.

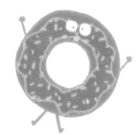

First on stage comes an Indian Samosa.

From behind the scenes sounded:

'Za ostra, po jej zjedzeniu aż gile lecą z nosa!'

The three pig judges, after annoying snorts and disputes
finally ask Samosa to explain her family roots.

She knows the ingredients of her stuffing,
but of her origin, she knows absolutely nothing.

Next to perform are the British instant noodles,
competing against their friends - Bavarian apple strudels.

They are slim and fit, extremely elastic,
proudly displaying their skills in artistic gymnastics.

Their names are Tom, Eric and Johnny.

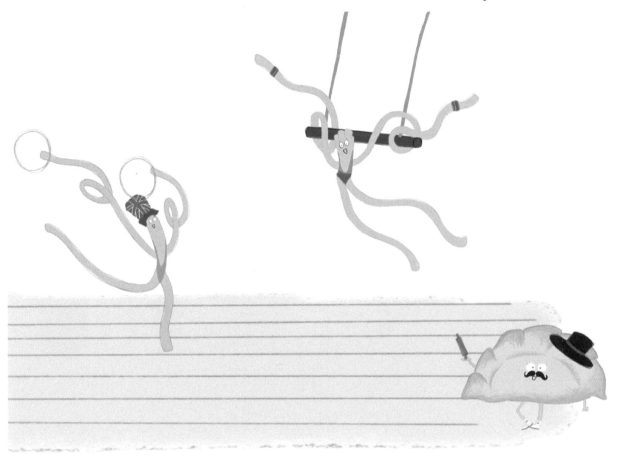

'Kto to widział, w chińskich zupkach anglosaskie makarony?'

Now it's time for the dough with the best chance of a win.

The one and only Prawn Dumpling, queen of Asian cuisine.

She is stylish, trendy, even gluten free.

That's exactly how everyone wants her to be.

Gently steamed, filled with shrimp and Chinese cabbage,
dipped in soy, isn't that a most delicious package!

'Bezglutenowa panienka, też mi rewelacja.
Bez glutenu, to żadna syta kolacja.'

One judge cried: 'What on Earth! Who is saying that?
Bring this joker on stage, let's see what he's got!'

Mr Pig and his wife, with her younger sister,
stare with amazement, when under the stage lights,
Pieróg Włodek looks even crispier.

'Hello, bonjour, buenos dias, aloha!

Dzień dobry, witam wszystkich, Jestem Pieróg Włodek
z pięknego Wałbrzycha.
Jestem zrobiony z ziemniaków, mąki, wody, sera, jajek i cebuli.
Podany z odrobiną oleju, wedle przepisu Babuni.

'I'm multilingual, that's my SECRET POWER.

I'm delicious, best eaten warm, within an hour'.

The audience loved what they'd heard and they'd seen,
they were very impressed with this Polish cuisine.

The judges had to take appropriate action,
and award the championship to Włodek.
There really was no other option.

"So, what's the moral of this story?" someone asks,

respect your roots,

know your background,

learn other languages -

to go far in life, just follow these simple tasks.

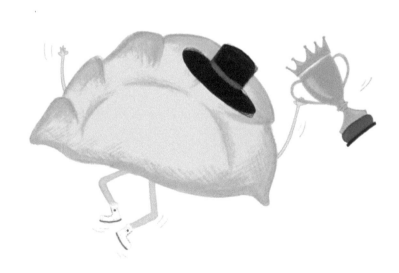

Visual Dictionary

	English	Polish	Phonetic
	Mobile phone	Telefon	te'lefon
	Hand bag	Torebka	to'repka
	Hat	Kapelusz	ka'peloosh
	Hair band	Opaska	o'pascka
	Shoes	Buty	'booti

	English	Polish	Phonetic
	Glasses	Okulary	okoolarɨ
	Bow tie	Muszka	'mooshka
	Trophy	Trofeum	Tro'pheoom
	Moustache	Wąsy	vousɨ
	Milk	Mleko	'mlecko

	English	Polish	Phonetic
	Apple	Jabłko	'yabwcko
	Flag	Flaga	'flaga
	Cookie	Ciastko	'tsyastcko
	Waffles	Gofry	'gofrɨ
	Doughnut (Donut)	Pączek	'powcheck

	English	Polish	Phonetic
	Chair	Krzesło	ksheswo
	Curtain	Kurtyna	koor'tyna
	Stage	Scena	s'tcena
	Fork	Widelec	Vi'delets
	Knife	Nóż	'noosh

	English	Polish	Phonetic
	Plate	Talerz	'talesh
	Onion	Cebula	ce'boola
	Rolling pin	Wałek	'vaweck
	Eggs	Jajka	'yaycka
	Bowl	Miska	'miscka

	English	Polish	Phonetic
	Potatoes	Ziemniaki	Zyem'nyakee
	Oil	Olej	'oley
	Water	Woda	'voda
	Flour	Mąka	'mowcka
	Cottage Cheese	Twaróg	'tfaroock

	English	Polish	Phonetic
	Map	Mapa	'mapa
	Wild pig	Dzik	'dzeeck
	Gingerbread	Piernik	py'erneeck
	Bear	Niedźwiedź	ny'edzvyetc
	Stork	Bocian	'botseean

	English	Polish	Phonetic
	Wolf	Wilk	'veelck
	European Bison	Żubr	'ʒoobr
	Roe Deer	Sarna	'sarna
	Boat	Łódź	wootɕ
	Dumplings	Pierogi	pye'rogee

About the Author

Anna Nassif was born in 1983, in Gorzow, Poland. She is a political scientist by education, however, since she became a resident of Sydney in 2008, she has been working as a music and piano teacher and has been involved in many community events.

She is a mother of three children.

She loves travel, ocean views and the taste of her grandma's dumplings. The publication of this story is the first step in realising Anna's dreams and goals, large and small.

Previous Publications:

"My Emigration" ("Moja Emigracja") as part of the 'My Emigration' literary competition, Favoryta Publishing House, 2012.

"Friday the thirteenth" ("Piątek Trzynastego") as part of the international literary competition "One Day. Poland, as I remember", Favoryta Publishing House, 2014.

Urodzona w Polsce w 1983 roku, Gorzowianka. Z zawodu, wykształcona muzycznie pianistka. Z wykształcenia, zawodowy politolog. Od 2008 roku mieszkanka Sydney, zawodowo związana z nauczaniem gry na fortepianie, społecznie aktywna w ramach licznych polonijnych projektów. Matka trójki dzieci. Miłośniczka podróży, widoku oceanu i smaku babcinych pierogów. Marzycielka, która tym opowiadaniem, od teraz właśnie, zaczyna wprowadzać w życie swoje mniejsze i większe marzenia.

Publikacje:

„Moja Emigracja" w ramach konkursu literackiego „Moja Emigracja", Wydawnictwo Favoryta 2012.

„Piątek Trzynastego" w ramach międzynarodowego konkursu literackiego „Jeden Dzien. Polska, jaka pamiętam", Wydawnictwo Favoryta 2014.

www.facebook.com/hissecretpower

Lightning Source UK Ltd.
Milton Keynes UK
UKHW052149070519
342251UK00001B/18/P